For Mum.

And to each word…

OH, SNOW LION,

You represent power and strength, fearlessness and joy.

Those who take the plunge are freer in the mind than those who circle around the pool of uncertainty and then give up trying.

You are never going to give up.

I want to help you see the beauty I saw aged sixteen, where I stumbled upon the vastness of the page, with all the colours of the rainbow which I collected as armoury to show a mirror of myself on the blank array of vastness which would cement me as an artist in the making at such a young age.

There was no fear.

There was intrigue, curiosity and investigation.

Intrigue of what I could create on such a vast opportunity of space.

I call my blank canvas an opportunity; not a fear that puts me off even attempting to try.

I geared towards ancient Egypt - through the pyramids and to Cleopatra's eyes. I delved into a sunset of history that ascertained a wonder of the world.

The archeological notion of digging stayed with me.

I became myself in that time, knowing there was no fear of exploring whatever blank canvas I would find thereon; even to this day.

I made a subconscious commitment to myself from that day that a blank canvas was my friend, and somewhat twenty years later, I still marvel in all that it gives me.

How amazing would it be to do that with each part of life?

There is such an opportunity to problem solve on an empty space; give it meaning and show the world what you're made of.

Even in times of hardship, the learning curve is immense.

Take the plunge without any trepidation of onlookers and their perceptions; those are a given of cause and effect; action and reaction.

The beauty of true art is to hold a true mirror to what's within you out into the world, and allow the world to make its own judgement.

The reader is free to hate your view of the world. The cinema goer can give you a bad review. The one who attends an exhibition can tilt their head at your art in confusion, and the best thing about it is that it's all valid, and very much needed.

We need the critic, the confused, the well-wisher, and the cynic alike.

We are all creative individuals, and we must embrace them all.

For when our art meets their perception, we understand the world much better.

When our mirror is held up, it reflects their true selves too.

We get very afraid to hold our true selves up on show, because we are unsure of how we will be seen.

This is the way of the world, and not in our control.

It is the process of life.

For us, dear Snow Lion, we must commit to the plunge of creativity and let the art take its course.

Take with you my words.

Don't be afraid to dig.

WORDS

Word on the street is... all words have different meanings.

They land sunny side up. Or even heads down.

It's unclear what they mean until they land.

For the process of 'start' and 'end' have different levels of meanings and understandings.

There is no end though, the end is the start.

Sshhhhh... don't tell the dictionary.

Whichever one you pick up....

ONE

POWER

SEESAW

Your voice rose to silence mine,

A seesaw in full flow.

I became grounded in decline,

Off to the clouds you chose.

But what goes up, must come down,

As the old saying goes.

Gravity is my friend true,

It will be yours too,

When your feet touch that rose.

I'M happy to be grounded

On the muddy field of real.

We're a wave rising and crashing in rhyme,

In reality you must feel.

I went away a little shattered,

It was your day today.

My voice is wonderfully still there,

It'll be there come what may.

A small battle is yours for now,

But today I won a war.

Knowing my voice is not lost,

It merely touched the floor.

HUMAN

A needed reminder.

I'm human,

You're human too.

Regardless of life,

This reminder anchors you.

When the clock strikes twelve, remember,

January arrives after December.

And after so long,

The reminder will sing that song.

The body starts to heal,

Don't dwell too long.

On a time once gone,

In reality you must feel.

TRUTH

The truth extraction.

Solidifies your stance.

Your existence plays a struggling chord,

And you move a happy dance.

Never the popular narrative to win over a mass,

But it is necessary for the world to see

But it still blames you, alas.

The truth should difficult,

And it should be delivered harsh.

It should take you on a thorny path,

In a charcoal marsh.

Let time take its course,

Let me tell you,

Let the truth be the force.

DEWS

We are a world in jigsaws.

Of rational raws.

Logical dews.

Create anew.

Build your shapes.

Build your path.

Rejoice in the aftermath.

JUDGEMENT

The guest was arriving imminently,

The house needed order.

The breath and sound of a voice had judgement.

For that there was no border.

It felt wrong to put on a show,

To save oneself from constant critique.

But it felt necessary to sort the mess

And to completely avoid the bleak.

She needed an adequate view.

Of a house she struggled to keep anew.

She could keep the blame at bay,

And she didn't heed to convention,

Come what may.

She wasn't losing herself for a phase,

It was the zen required that kept her in praise.

All the guest came for was some chai and advice.

Then she looked at herself,

Thought about it twice.

She started giving herself advice.

Nothing is perfect for him it seems,

Then why did his critique so beam?

Her home is her safety,

Away from the world.

It's not for others to understand

Nor for abuse to be hurled.

Maintain your home,

For what it does.

Self-care is a must,

Let it create a buzz.

PEAKS

Compliments are things,

We seem to fear.

They are a test,

They seem to cheer.

How you handle them,

How you keep them abreast.

Refrain from the peaks,

Not close to your chest.

For there may be a devil at work,

Not all compliments are meant as such,

In some, the shaitan may lurk.

IMPOSTER

How can we tame a syndrome?

When we feel like imposters in our own home?

Our posterior made its mark,

On the sofa we bought.

But to navigate the dark,

We still need to be taught.

We've fought over the channels,

We wanted to desperately view.

And yet, here we are,

Patiently waiting in a queue.

Asking ourselves if we belong,

If we're allowed to sing the same song.

We still have the key to the front door,

And we understand the laminate floor.

Imposter we are definitely not.

The soul is marked by a dot.

IMMIGRANT

Should we agitate to debate and educate?

Or should we agitate to hate?

We must put the shoes of anger at the door.

Before we step on the temple floor.

Grace in the flow of moving forward.

And grace in the verbatim asking for your word.

There is nothing sweeter than the Zoroastrian Parsi's tale.

For days past in the journey,

A resolve from where they set sail.

The Zoroastrian arrived merely,

To better the land he met.

Then to invade an isle with ideology

That ends in a sacred threat.

SERVE

To the one dismissed from existence for asking a probe.

What in education, experience and attitude do you know?

'Quite a bit', kind Sir.

'I am the one you serve, as a pro.

If I am silenced in your quest to reach a height.

I'll judge your intention.

In there, there is might in plain sight'.

PAST

Some people feel I live in North West London.

But I have lived in the past too much.

Now the station's passed away.

I'm not grieving it as such.

I'm free of a way of living,

That brought me to my knees.

I felt tired of being sugarcane.

For people to use me as they pleased.

I was accommodating like a hotel chain.

I was forever always there.

But when I saw my own humanity.

The arena had laid bare.

They preferred the carpet I became.

When I didn't put up a fight.

But now when I'm myself.

None are in my sight.

The ones who are there are the gems.

The others can stay away.

I'll always choose myself.

Living the lifelong day.

BLIND

With the day, we have the same.

But what happens when speed takes place?

Who do I sit and blame?

I thought my astigmatic vision,

Was the only blindness I had.

Until I understood I respected time,

But blindness made me sad.

I function a bit differently,

But I know when I'm in the zone.

I know I reside on Earth too.

So a schedule I have to hone.

There's nothing wrong with a bit of difference.

For the norm is there to be shown.

When new, undiscovered things are implemented.

Minds are certainly blown.

Keep all judgments where you should.

Away and completely at bay.

I'll keep my mind, my blindness and all,

I'll take it any day.

RIGHT

If you misspell right for write,

You're really not wrong.

The truth in the pen is correct.

And you're writing your own song.

You're speaking your own truth,

With your own words.

So right or write,

Are in the same herd.

Don't worry about the stumble.

The right to write and to right the wrong

are part of the same grumble.

EVE

When Eve arrived first,

We spoke of Newton and Jobs.

Eve claimed first,

As Adam's heart throbs.

We must never forget.

That Eve arrives before tomorrow.

Eve ended her way

In naivety and sorrow.

But the claim on the apple,

Is for all to see.

It was not man.

For it was she.

So now, why is Eve so eager

To find a way in the modern play?

When she should remember,

Eve happens,

Before the next day.

SQUARE

A square with corners.

We remain at our end.

We link our own border.

We make it our friend.

We play tug of war.

With our truth in its might.

But we never really understand.

Their truth in plain sight.

We must meet in the middle.

If evolution is what we want.

If we remain stagnant.

We must always stop the front.

We virtue signal our way.

Into a moral high ground.

But the character we build.

Puts our truth in compound.

FOUR

Why did two plus two end up four?

Were we so afraid to say no?

Were we so exhausted from the back and forth?

We accepted the status quo?

CIRCLE

The circular edges ascended towards the sky.

Everyone's gaze saw the coin fly up high.

Their vision matched the movement of the coin.

All were in tangent, and all did join.

There was an equal chance of either side,

Landing on the floor.

Whichever faced down and out,

The other held the door.

There was a sign of what was to come,

Who started off the race.

But neither really could deny,

The other one had grace.

QUESTION

'Who must I owe it to?'

She needed a clue

'Myself?

She asked.

'Yes!'

They gasped.

'I much prefer it away from me.

It always feeds the glee.'

'But whenever you have.'

They proclaimed.

'You fell to the ground.

And suffered in pain.

Be a trapeze artist.

Be that balancing act.

You know you need to help yourself.

And that stating is a fact.'

DISRUPT

If disruption was nowhere near

Where would we be?

Is it so clear?

We need a force to cut through the dirt.

To make it through.

In controversy it flirts.

Disruption drills past

The zen of the quo.

Not the one who

Disturbs the flow.

We need to disrupt

To see new ideals.

We will get excited

Have all the feels.

Dr King and Gandhi

Paved the way.

In the current

They did not stay.

We often discard

Differences of the state.

But what disruption does

Is give us a clean slate.

PAUSE

Does the sky get burnt when the sun is so fierce?

TWO

STRENGTH

NOISE

What does silence sound like?

When you're trying to scream?

You're incarcerated into your mind,

It's not even a dream.

Everyone is silencing you,

You're trying to express.

The words don't make sense,

The tears try their best.

What does silence look like?

The blindfold over your speech.

The silence is feeling failure.

Slowly it must creep.

What does silence sound like?

When you're bellowing for aid.

When you're trying to make others comprehend.

It's a heavy price you've paid.

REST

'Please rest.'

She said.

She stumbled across the room.

The table knocked,

And she felt a sense of doom.

'Please rest'

She collapsed and stopped.

She couldn't find a softer landing,

And on the floor she dropped.

'Please rest.'

She said,

Again and again.

She realised just one part.

All the words of support,

Were all hers from the start.

MOTHERHOOD

Mum was asked why

Focus was away from her.

She got annoyed.

A conversation she tried to deter.

Her eyes glistened.

I saw the real.

A mask of mamta.

A really big deal.

A motherhood of being.

I feel I was seeing.

Her way in which

To shield me through.

The pain of life

Was really strife.

And it really was

A mother's cue.

GANDHARI

We take lessons from epic tales

In the Kurukshetra War.

A time when Truth be told,

Truth was on the floor.

I see Gandhari as a woman to explore.

She couldn't see,

In which she chose to ignore.

The plight of the sight

When destruction came to her door.

Had she felt more towards

The sons than to the spouse

Maybe evolution could have avoided destruction,

And not burnt down her house.

A lineage continue in good faith,

Of which she could be proud.

But instead she saw a line of support,

To which she had vowed.

She lost all hundred sons to combat,

None of whom survived.

She hadn't seen destruction in plain view.

But a wailing mother cried.

I often wonder what could occur,

Had she seen everything first.

Maybe the war could have been averted,

And history wouldn't have been so cursed.

BLIND

Maya Yashoda lovingly portrays,

A constant state of strength.

Her love for our LordKrishna

Has infintely no defined length.

Her motherly love and mamta,

Is a clear sign of warmth.

But we need to stop ourselves

And really ask henceforth.

When does the boundary of blindness

Seep its way through?

When you don't want to hear

A different kind of view?

What if the person's help

Was intentionally due?

And they were merely trying to aid,

The battle within you?

Moving away from mamta here

Wasn't really on the cards.

But thinking with your brain and heart,

Ensures your decision placards.

ZONE

'You should try new things.'

'You have the knack.'

'Why hold yourself back?'

She said, with a message to hone.

Whilst she sat,

Relaxing in her comfort zone.

PRAY

'How are you?'

She asked.

After a hiatus away.

'I'm doing the work,

I clean in the evening,

I sleep all day.

There is work still to do.

It's hard,

But I'm not cutting a corner.

It's a good job,

My name means to pray.'

STONES

The beans diluted themselves

In hot boiling water.

Immersing in the path they chose,

Like I must do, a daughter.

The path so far made no sense.

And the waves a mild tension tense.

The path had a thorn and rose,

But now I bathe in flow and prose

Suddenly it all seems clear.

My knowledge flowed,

My learning fear,

Disappeared.

Stones were set,

But now they seem

To place their bets.

On all my dreams.

PEN

Who is my 3am friend?

It's 3am now.

I'm up, wondering

Who can I turn to?

I'm here, completely fine,

With no sleep deprived.

But thoughts kept me up,

And completely derived.

I'm here.

At 3am.

So the page is my friend.

My go to for all.

It's the pen in the end.

YEAR

Silence and patience are your true friends.

They continue you on a path of true ends.

When chaos strikes, feel all you need.

But accept it as growth needs a feed.

For you know now what's in store for you.

To the past you have bidded adieu.

It's only when a door closes in.

That you realise how lucky you've been.

To leave the torturing nature of a place.

That you're now free to roam in grace.

It is hard to understand this much,

But truth must prevail and prevail, it does such.

There was a time that all focus was on one.

But now you're free from a cage that weighed a ton.

There is hope in the unknown at the turn of a year,

There's a tranquil essence, and there is no fear.

For you know you left this place giving it your all.

And it felt all assumed you'd fall.

Butterflies don't fall in place.

They flap their wings and move in grace.

Heaven forbid those who think,

That they'll collapse, fall and sink.

It's an amazing feeling to lose so much.

I'd rather it not be my crutch.

I'm grateful for the lessons I've learnt.

The growth despite the feelings of burns.

The scabs are armoury to take with me through,

At the turn of the year, refreshed and new.

Thank you all for the harshest of fears.

You keep your might,

I'll keep my year.

MAP

A Treasure map each time I wake up.

A path to navigate to show I've shown up.

A day in my mind is taxing to say the least.

If I don't tick the list, I've fed the beast.

Heaven forbid, I end up all day.

By ticking off the first point in dismay.

I will lose myself in a dream in the rising Sun.

I'll look not to win the day,

But proclaim the day has won.

And for the rest of the time.

My only crime

Is that I didn't keep my anxiety aligned.

I am trying my hardest not to drop a plate.

But everyday, I know I'll need a cleaner slate.

Starting again,

There seems to be no end.

On this path of flow,

I'll proclaim,

It drives me round the bend.

There are no excuses here,

Just endless attempts.

Please never judge anyone

Nor make them exempt.

BRAVERY

There was a moment of understanding.

Through all the flags pointing towards forever.

But I could never understand the bravery needed,

For this harsh, yet beautiful, unequivocal endeavour.

CAUTION

Finding out Santa wasn't real.

History books with biases were no big deal.

The placement of you on Earth mattered most.

It presented you with the way of thought from the host.

Nothing was ever a matter of fact.

A lot was staged, a very long act.

I still trust in hope and happier beings.

But I am more cautious with whom I'm dealing.

I have taken a few blows of misjudgements, true.

But I am faithful yet, in reading the true you.

BENCH

I'm here.

They're here.

The tears are flowing.

My eyes are moist.

My face is glowing.

I'm sullen in despair of that past.

But I remember the lesson.

It comes back fast.

The way to move is forward to.

The place that's yet to be with you.

Revolutions don't need wars in a bad sense.

They can be for positive change.

A seat on the bench.

CLAW

The hardest lesson was once a stepping stone.

There came a bitter blow.

But if it didn't teach you,

You really didn't grow.

With each knock there comes a test.

You knew you were never your best,

In all the places you were before.

But now your here,

With lesser fear,

Climbing claw by claw.

MOMENTUM

The line was at length,

All had their turn.

They took the leap,

A new life she did yearn.

She slowly moved along with the herd,

Orderly being the operative word.

British by definition,

But not like the condition.

She reached the front,

Once before.

The shutter closed,

Followed by the door.

She thought it was the end,

To a long winded road.

But she took it as a sign to send,

A unique and wonderful code.

To try again and join the cue,

This time, she thought,

Her attempt was due.

The shutter lowered,

And the door screeched.

The end of the line,

She had almost reached.

She picked up pace,

Fear in her heart.

But made it still,

She played her part.

The wings that grew,

The momentum brewed.

A new found freedom,

Spoke a song.

She never looked back,

Grace in tact,

To the old life once gone.

EXERCISE

The haven of exercise is seeing just women in the bay.

Maybe it's the time of day.

Maybe it's the sign of our times.

Whatever it is,

It's sublime.

MIGHT

A few painful shocks.

But persistence paved the way.

The law of evolution is beginning to play.

The movement of life continues.

Keeps naysayers at bay.

Keep a difference in your stance today.

Right foot forward.

Culture in sight.

Keep moving,

And lift with your might.

THREE

FEARLESSNESS

SCOPE

The right eye beaconed them,

To understand the need.

The pole was a mystery,

They were intrigued indeed.

There were a multitude of colours,

Then came solid shapes.

Patterns had emerged.

The curiosity rightly surged.

The pole responded on their cue,

To fill their eyes with a new design.

But their tired eyes came through,

And their enthusiasm declined.

The view was entertaining for a while,

But now they were getting annoyed.

They stopped turning the dial,

They began to completely avoid.

Creativity is to see what would appear,

But the colours began to disappear.

Creativity began to lose her way,

In her heart she didn't want to stay.

'Never mind' thought the tired pole,

'I'll return to my soul.

I'll keep my colours hidden 'til then.

I'll know when to start again'.

TORNADO

A tornado struck,

Took with it the roof.

The house was on tenterhooks,

The foundation aloof.

The wind has been strong,

With a force not wrong.

But the foundation hasn't gone,

It's still in song.

Singing the hymn it needs,

To fulfil its deeds.

Patience awaits,

The fixing of gates.

You must look at yourself,

At the end of the day,

Knowing you fought,

Your demons away.

If you stand alone,

With the wreckage of being,

Know that you did right by freeing.

All the pent up anger and rage,

It was a sign to build on the foundations and gauge.

What mattered most in your life all along,

Keep building it up,

And singing that song.

UNLOCK

Each Monday, I sat and explained how I felt.

I picked apart the hand I was dealt.

She made me see a new way in thought.

I saw in my own mind I'd be caught.

I sat there looking in dismay.

But she showed me a path,

A different type of way.

I saw much salt water during the time,

Though I felt it,

It felt sublime.

The language I spoke so far in turn.

It had its place,

But I had to be stern.

Finally I felt I could put it all down.

The luggage I carried,

I didn't drown.

'Speak', she said.

'Let it all out'.

'Trust me' she said,

'Remove all doubt'.

The words transpired,

The knot unlocked.

'How do you feel?'

'I feel',

I clocked.

MAGGIE

Follow Maggie as she stumbles.

And continues to get up.

There's so much to learn from cartoons.

Keeping going,

Sums it up.

Maggie is the one to assess.

Never let the focus digress.

She shows you how to live your life.

Get up whether success or strife.

DAWN

What do we claim a circular form?

We laugh when night becomes dawn.

The words and art that kept you afloat.

Environments you made,

But were yours to quote.

Nothing brings you back down to earth,

Like finding meaning about your birth.

You were not here merely to quote.

You really needed to burn that boat.

You had to bring the canvas back,

And realise there was your knack.

Reclaim the game of living life,

Else chaos will enter and turn the knife.

What do we claim a circle to be?

The work that allows you to be free.

EMERGE

The red light glared,

She knew it was time.

To put on a break,

To see a formed line.

Of everything she held so dear.

Seem to simply and quickly disappear.

She sat with this feeling.

Quietly observing.

Something which she hadn't done before.

Why was this left

So late in the day?

She still went about the chore.

A path emerged.

She geared towards the road.

From a lost soul

In the deep jungle.

The complexity showed.

She did the work needed until now.

A requirement of society.

She didn't bow.

But a few words from an old guide stuck.

`We're always made to be the carer,

We must never duck'.

Us women have the power.

It really hits home

And it really does suck.

Go find your inner power.

No one can take that from you.

In strength you must shower.

PIVOT

Legend says we have multiple hands

In all the photos I've seen.

We epitomise multi-tasking.

And we're often the reigning queen.

But today is a day I realise,

I don't want the history I made.

To determine a future I can write.

I'll choose where my hat will be laid.

All made their weird judgments,

Of actions and words once said.

But we write our paths everyday,

An evolution we'll write instead.

A tired mind,

All battered and bruised.

Such battle scars,

Now make me amused.

I'll look to this year as a pivot,

As I deem fit.

I often wondered whilst standing tall,

Where on earth I would sit.

I'm here today due to all who had my back.

Whether related by blood,

Or a time once gone,

Their energy kept me on track.

I've learnt so much of life in all

Of the last few years at least.

The mental hurdles are overcome,

A battle and a beast.

An air of tranquillity,

I'm calmer in life too.

I take each day with gratitude,

And look towards anew.

CHOICE

I learnt the meaning of those words didn't exist,

And it was music to one's ear.

I'll take my life as a lesson

From all who cannot cheer.

Move to a life of choice,

However hard it is akin.

Always have a focussed vision.

Always look within.

UNSTOPPABLE

Must the fear be of spiders, ghouls or bills?

Which one holds us to ransom the most?

Which stops us from being unstoppable?

Those deserve a ghost.

LEADER

A global front with a fractured soul.

The same test and the same mutations.

All expose the leadership of control.

And how it moved in gestation.

We look to those who handled the task at hand.

And judge on how they helped their land.

For strength, leadership, and the same.

It's easy for us all to place the blame.

But leadership is a test of you.

From adversity you must take your cue.

When all is well,

There's no debate.

All and sundry will seem so great.

Your test as head of any state,

Is how you treat those

Who earn less weight.

I'm happy I live in developed times.

But I know I'm blessed with locational rhymes.

The history books will always be biased bound.

But truth will be told from our hearts,

Minds and every sound.

There is dismay at leadership every day.

They've gone for the children, doctors

And the dismantling of the UK.

STAGE

I peered from the wings.

The stage was lit.

Darkness hid in plain sight.

I heard some words

From the mood,

And day turned into night.

The lights were on the stage,

A bare space made,

A canvas there laid.

I moved towards central stage.

I lost the feeling of a cage.

I moved around in flow thereon.

I forgot all eyes were peering on.

Listening to the song once gone.

Suddenly the music dropped.

My heart started to beat so high.

The feet just stopped dancing,

And let out a long silent sigh.

There came a roaring applause and cheer,

Then Suddenly came end of fear.

All who watched got on their feet,

No one was sitting on their seat.

I suddenly saw what all had said,

That fear was all in my head.

VALUES

She gazed at herself in the mirror,

After an age away.

She closed her eyes for a bit,

And looked in dismay.

There were some fears,

She could foresee.

But in what she saw,

She let things be.

The passing of time,

Held her close.

She did not feel ill,

Nor was she gross.

She let her eyes seep slowly through.

To marvel at the growth,

A mark of truth.

There was still a numbing feeling,

She hoped would go away.

She decided to keep her values high,

And keep her thoughts at bay.

OUTCOME

The dishes form an orderly queue,

They will get the rinse they were due.

I use my proven direction in a way,

It's like the dirt is being kept at bay.

The process seems to do the trick,

I'll continue today even though I'm sick.

I cannot fathom an outcome at all,

But I won't let the effort fall.

I cannot control the outcome herewith,

If you control it, there is a myth.

We tend to want to control the win,

But you see, chasing an outcome is a sin.

WALK

We have ourselves a long walk too.

Not the kind Mandela was due.

It's less a signal of a change in the world.

It's more of a notion that needs to be hurled.

It's more the need to move your lazy bum.

When you honour the fact that sedentary is glum.

The beanie hat is on your head.

And out the door your feet have fled.

The need to walk is a daily event.

In your walking goal,

You make a small dent.

HOME

Brick by brick we stick together,

A home built from love.

Inch by inch we pave the way,

For warmth and peaceful doves.

Bit by bit the home becomes,

Familiar in the heart.

But then you know you've had a comfort

It hits you like a dart.

The home itself tires out itself

From always cocooning you inside.

Make sure you maintain its wonderment,

But don't make it a wasteful plight.

It's easy to stay stagnant,

When there is no dilemma.

But remember standing still,

Is death on you forever.

DUTY

The tarpaulin was sitting idle,

Waiting patiently to be of use.

Like those majdoors on Mumbai's roadside,

Waiting to serve a truce.

A motherly concern came from inside,

That the tarpaulin needed cover.

I sat there wondering before making a move,

Whether it was the dutiful endeavour.

To take the rain from the Gods,

And protect the vulnerable things.

It seems it is at odds,

On what its duty brings.

In all this thought the heavens decided,

It no longer could,

Hold off for any action taken,

It had its own duty,

As it surely would.

The tarpaulin got soaked in water,

The heavens didn't mind,

But the tarpaulin again fulfilled its duty,

For the furniture in kind.

FREEDOM

In the state to meditate.

We must walk through fear.

The sun has set,

The path is dark,

The road is still not clear.

We know there seems to be a freedom,

In which we are caught,

But even in the darkest night,

I see the stars that fiercely fought.

I realise there is no end,

The sun will rise in time.

But for now the moon,

At the end of today

Really is sublime.

HEROINE

A battle for respect,

What happens when this truth is found?

We look back at our youth,

We are left well bound.

By sight we see a different prose.

From victimhood,

A heroine rose.

We take towards a new dialogue,

We no longer need a demagogue.

We still hold those events so dear,

But bitterness we do not fear.

For it was a lesson to be learned,

For now a new found freedom earned.

We see maturity seeping in,

To the cracks in our vision,

It's no longer a sin.

SOLITUDE

The hand was dealt,

There was no tear.

The lessons came,

An impending fear.

But through the pace,

I walked along,

A path I made,

I sang my song.

To calm myself,

From despair,

Of not knowing,

What was in the air.

I realise now,

What was going on.

Through adversity,

The sun has shone.

I moved away from external means,

I realised internally itself it cleans.

Once you embrace silence and solitude,

You understand your every molecule.

FOUR

JOY

HIATUS

Hiatuses are hilarious.

They are so weird.

I don't understand,

They almost disappeared.

You return again,

But you're not really you.

You changed a bit,

You knew it was due.

You are there today,

Taking stock.

Glad of moving on,

You don't feel on the dock.

There's no attachment,

That you held dear.

You arrived here certain,

You can only cheer.

ZEN

My jaw was unclenched,

There was no ache.

Freedom began,

To overtake.

Yesterday seemed so sour,

Today I want to devour.

We keep coming to the end of the year,

Let us take stock and cheer.

We look back at the things,

We took for granted.

For the seeds in thought,

that we had planted.

Today though,

I sit on the floor.

Thank all the closed doors.

I feel a sense of ultimate zen.

I'm really glad,

Of the effort added then.

Barriers shattered,

Cycles battered,

Toxicity shown the door.

Suddenly I felt,

The life I'm dealt,

Isn't heavy anymore.

BRICKS

Evening set,

The fiddler played,

His violin in disdain.

All arrived at their balconies,

To understand his pain.

All were lost in the sweet sounds,

When he saw his play in vain.

A small applause grew,

Against the bars.

The crowd drew,

Glistening against moon and stars.

He tipped his hat,

Sheepishly smiled,

But he realised,

It took him a while,

To understand his play,

Was a calling for much more,

Then they had to say.

As he walked down the staircase

He noticed each solid brick,

He never realised their presence before.

He went for a warm embrace.

He touched each brick in gratitude,

For all their help and support.

He realised he wasn't in solitude,

As he had previously thought.

The house had seen so many things,

So many storms before.

It kept being nurtured to greater heights,

you could touch the sky much more.

When he looked up from the ground,

He saw the moon and stars.

He thanked all that came before him,

Who helped him find the bars.

A lesson here for all of us,

We see art in all its glory.

But look at what has happened so far,

And you see the fuller story.

PLANTED

It's an unclear how this point was met,

I'm trying to remember.

Planting seems to be necessary,

When tulips see December.

A platform here where we're free to be,

One I don't take for granted.

I'm happy the seeds that dug,

Have naturally been planted.

The number of words matter less right here,

It matters more what they mean.

When all seemed lost,

I saw that,

Writing found a way.

Drawing came a surprising second,

But expression all the way.

There were surprises at the last attempt,

Realities shown all around.

I'm ready for what this version brings,

I'll take in every sound.

I'll see the real for the ones that critique,

I simply cannot wait.

Anyone who has shown their soul,

Surely can relate.

ROOTS

Roots there,

But feet here.

How must you make your bed?

From which angle must you start?

Which parts of culture must you shed?

For a hit and miss,

For what is deemed

Ethically right?

And whose perception,

When we judge this stance

Is truly in plain sight?

It's an approach to take,

For evolution's sake,

That you bring with you the norm.

All by which traditions to keep,

And which really must be gone.

There's a fear from those before us here,

That we'll lose the grip on the tide.

But they need to remember a chorus cheer,

Isn't a verse in pride.

We must make our own music,

With the notes they handed over.

We may have brought a new found way.

At the white cliffs of Dover.

OAK

How easy it is to breathe,

After you've held on for too long.

How the feeling of release,

Brings you to belong.

You sit on the muddy field,

Of really all you know.

And are grateful for the plants,

You nature and you sow.

The rain and sun need equal measure,

One for sorrow,

The other for pleasure.

You will grow an oak

With the battles you've won.

You'll take the pages,

And hide from the sun.

Highly, the tree will grow,

Well done for saying that difficult no.

There is a way in which,

The trunk doesn't break.

When adversity strikes,

It'll move and shake.

But break it won't.

It knows the score.

You rise,

By touching the floor.

FLOWERS

Rayners Lane alongside Pinner,

Is not just a walk in the park.

Following signs proclaiming 'this way',

Help to navigate the dark.

But to walk along that street,

A complexity seeks,

Often look towards the council estate.

With the police car flashing before your eyes,

Flowers bloom at its gate.

There is something for the critical thinker,

And not merely the blind mouse.

One will end up in a dead end,

The other will find their house.

COLOURS

Flowers gone.

Blooms weren't there.

Colours gone.

Does it seem fair?

There was just mud,

An important start.

But there's no bud,

The colours depart?

A mood seems to stay,

But I returned again,

Later that day.

Colour seemed to be restored,

The colours really hit a chord.

PINK

A balloon hovered like a shade,

Covering the glowing Sun.

She held onto it because it was a balloon,

And they made life so fun.

It was laced with pink glitter,

And all the things that made her see,

Back to a life with no issues,

All there was, was glee.

The string was in her grip,

And she held on for dear life.

She didn't know what would happen,

If the balloon was out of sight.

She felt at home in its grace,

And letting go she wouldn't face.

But a tug of wind arrived,

The balloon began to stir.

She tried so long to hold on,

Her hopes began to blur.

Her response seemed so fawn,

She had to save the pink,

But before too long,

Her heart began to sink.

She let go of the string,

She saw failure she repelled.

But what freedom did it bring?

She could never tell.

Something came over her,

a new feeling began to fold.

She was weirdly happy,

She let go of the hold.

She began to smile,

And was free of denial.

That there was life without her pink balloon.

Little did she know,

That when you grow,

Growth happens so soon.

A freedom drew a breath,

in every single vein.

A joyous feeling rushed in,

It started to engrain.

She took a few steps forward,

She felt lighter in her stance.

She realised a life awaited,

She began to move and dance.

There is joy in letting go of things,

That no longer serve.

In freedom there is might,

A freedom you deserve.

ORANGE

The rain refrained.

The orange arrived.

I wasn't betrayed.

The Sun wasn't revived.

It was the clouds that formed the mellow.

A burnt type of scented yellow.

An orange cloud arrived again,

But now I saw a new type of zen.

SURPRISE

It'll rain again this evening it seems.

It's eerily beautiful.

And hauntingly predictable.

Yet is spell bounding beyond surprise.

FLY

'I was never first.

Did you mind'

'No', she said.

Surprise a find.

'I wanted you to be with all.

But never so high where the fall was tall.

It mattered more that you were no less.

That was the aim in which I could bless.

You are with all that strength I gave,

But never did you once cave.

Now you need to find your own,

I did my work,

For you have flown.'

BOND

The length of the bond was known to us,

From when we first marked this track.

We now have seen so much of one another,

We might know every hack.

We see things through a similar lens,

Though our lives may be poles apart.

But we agree when cooking pasta,

That capsicum should be sautéed at the start.

MAMTA

Not so many hugs,

The warmth came from the chai.

She may never praise all the good,

I looked at her and sighed.

I saw the praise in the next role,

To make better my life through.

That's when I learnt a mother's love,

Was to see that progress grew.

I saw more warmth in the request,

To wrap up warm when cold.

She mentioned the sourdough was cheaper elsewhere,

She said never settle,

And be bold.

You really have to learn the dialect,

In which her heartstrings speak.

She really does tell you her love,

You can see it in the peaks.

DADDY

He sat in deep thought,

The mind wanted to completely sort.

All the things he wanted to say,

It was hard to keep his trepidation at bay.

There was a little human looking up at him,

He smiled back, but his heartstrings seemed too dim.

He wasn't keeping sadness at bay,

He wanted to write a story to say,

How he raised his daughter in his own way.

To narrate it when she understood,

But for now he knew all he could,

Do for her was to be her rock.

She looked up again and waved a tiny sock.

He knew she didn't understand it all.

Never mind, he thought.

The words will fall.

The reader will wait until she knew,

What each word meant,

And that Daddy's tale was true.

YET

Yet my friend.

Yet has no end.

I've not finished yet.

There's still time.

Yet my friend.

Yet lets the clock chime.

Yet is always there.

Yet has trust.

Yet, what a friend.

Yet is a must.

SONG

A layer died.

A paradox.

I'm still alive.

But the layer died.

An emotion left.

I feel such relief.

It felt so long,

But the phase was brief.

Life is a song.

There's no end in sight.

Fear not the unknown.

Keep flowing like a kite.

JIGSAW

All the pieces were together,

Finally, at last.

All of them fit forever,

As solid as stained glass.

A jigsaw saw borders with each tiny piece,

The perception of being broken,

Seemed to finally cease.

SOUL

Thank you for the fuel of doubt,

The journey was of sugar.

The header was where the aim felt I was,

But I ended up the footer.

The grounding that transpired from there,

Gave the game away.

It was from me to start again,

And to keep you all at bay.

There comes a time in one's life,

To really dig a hole.

To understand the core of being,

And to rekindle a lost soul.

Acknowledgments

None of this would have been possible without the Akimbo Workshops, founded by Seth Godin.

Writing in Community has been something of a transformational experience, taking me from anxiously curious human to a self-published author for a second time, and enabling me to become a lifelong writer.

Thank you to Kristin Hatcher & Angus Lockyer for their immense support, guidance and coaching.

To all of the WIC peers, especially the original Snow Lion, Mark, who paved the way for the title of this book.

And my creative peers in Pro6 as we complete 100 days of creativity to now moving onto even more.

Thank you to Nadine and Clear for being amazing beta readers, ready with their feedback and support during the editing process.

Thank you Hiral and Anjali, my lifelong friends who have stood by me during the toughest of times.

To my Mum, who I owe my life.

And to Lord Shiva, for the infinite curiosity to understand the inexplicable.

Also by Puja Teli

The Hill

www.wordsinprogress.uk/subscribe

Printed in Great Britain
by Amazon

80737868R10102